WRITER'S
TOOLBOX

It's All About You
Writing Your Own Journal

by Nancy Loewen

illustrated by Christopher Lyles and Todd Ouren

Picture Window Books
Minneapolis, Minnesota

Editor: Jill Kalz
Designer: Lori Bye
Page Production: Melissa Kes
Art Director: Nathan Gassman
Editorial Director: Nick Healy
Creative Director: Joe Ewest
The illustrations in this book were created digitally.

Picture Window Books
151 Good Counsel Drive
P.O. Box 669
Mankato, MN 56002-0669
877-845-8392
www.picturewindowbooks.com

Printed in the United States of America.

 All books published by Picture Window Books
are manufactured with paper containing at least
10 percent post-consumer waste.

Library of Congress Cataloging-in-Publication Data
Loewen, Nancy, 1964–
It's all about you : writing your own journal /
by Nancy Loewen ; illustrated by Christopher Lyles
and Todd Ouren.
p. cm. — (Writer's toolbox)
Includes index.
ISBN 978-1-4048-5520-5 (library binding)
ISBN 978-1-4048-5698-1 (paperback)
1. Diaries—Authorship—Juvenile literature. I. Lyles,
Christopher, 1977– ill. II. Ouren, Todd, ill. III. Title.
PN4390.L64 2009
808.06'692—dc22   2009003296

Special thanks to our adviser, Terry Flaherty, Ph.D., Professor of English, Minnesota State University, Mankato, for his expertise.

Imagine a place where you can say whatever you want. Whatever! And you can say it however you want.

There IS such a place. It's inside the pages of your very own journal.

A journal is a written record of your thoughts, feelings, and experiences. It's just for you—no one else should read it without your permission. A journal can take many forms: a blank book from a bookstore, a notebook, a file on a computer. The choice is yours!

Riley is a boy in the fourth grade. Let's take a peek inside his journal to learn more about how you can keep your own journal.

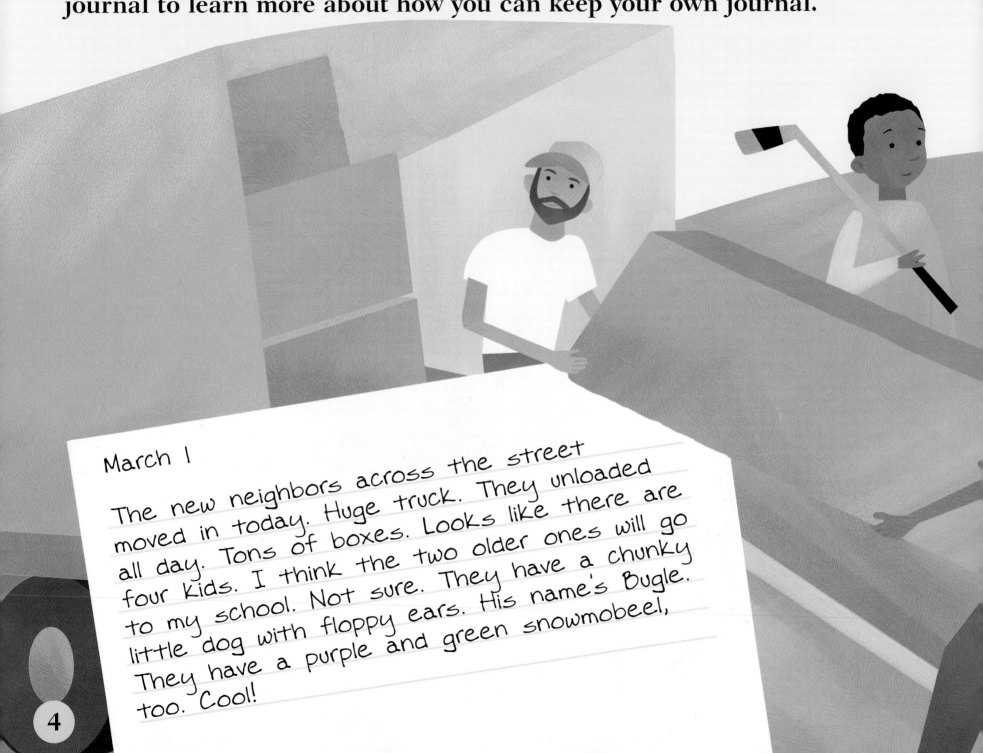

March 1

The new neighbors across the street moved in today. Huge truck. They unloaded all day. Tons of boxes. Looks like there are four kids. I think the two older ones will go to my school. Not sure. They have a chunky little dog with floppy ears. His name's Bugle. They have a purple and green snowmobeel, too. Cool!

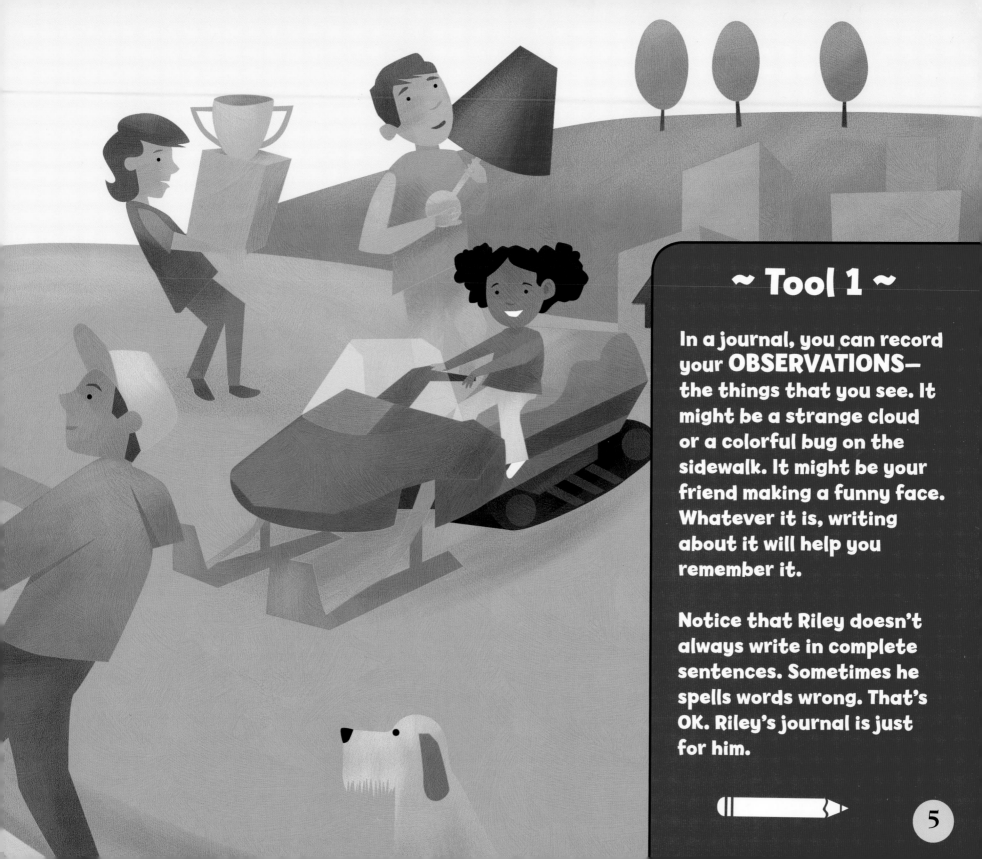

~ Tool 1 ~

In a journal, you can record your **OBSERVATIONS**— the things that you see. It might be a strange cloud or a colorful bug on the sidewalk. It might be your friend making a funny face. Whatever it is, writing about it will help you remember it.

Notice that Riley doesn't always write in complete sentences. Sometimes he spells words wrong. That's OK. Riley's journal is just for him.

~ Tool 2 ~

A journal is a good place to write down your **EMOTIONS**. It doesn't matter what those emotions are—sadness, anger, fear, excitement, happiness. Riley didn't play well today and is feeling really bad. Writing in a journal can be like talking to a good friend.

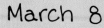

March 8

I tried out for the traveling baseball team today. Really worried I didn't make it. I dropped a fly ball and only got a couple good hits. Mr. Franklin was there taking notes. When we were leaving, he smiled at Dan, but he didn't smile at me. I'm feeling pretty bad right now.

7

March 10

Didn't make the traveling team. Dan made it. I can't believe it. I thought I did better than he did. And now I'm grounded because my sister says I pushed her. I barely touched her. It's not my fault she's so clumsy.

LIFE ISN'T FAIR!!!

March 13

Today I found out I'm on the in-house baseball team with Xavier and Jeff! I always have fun with them. I'm feeling better now. I just want to get out and play. Can't wait for practice tomorrow.

~ Tool 3 ~

If writing in a journal is a school assignment, you might be asked to use **WRITING PROMPTS.** Prompts are directions that help get your writing mind going. They're a great way to get started if you can't think of anything to write about.

March 27

What is your favorite part of the weekend?

My favorite part of the weekend is Friday, right when I get home from school. From 3:00 Friday to 8:00 Monday is 65 hours of no school! School is OK, but it's nice to have a break. Plus, we have pizza and movies on Friday nights. And Mom and Dad don't make me practice my trumpet. Fridays are great!

~ Tool 4 ~

Sometimes it's hard to get writing, even with a prompt. One way to get your words flowing again is to do **FREE WRITING**. In free writing, you write whatever pops into your head. You don't have to write in sentences. You don't even have to make sense. Just keep going, without stopping. You might be surprised at what you discover.

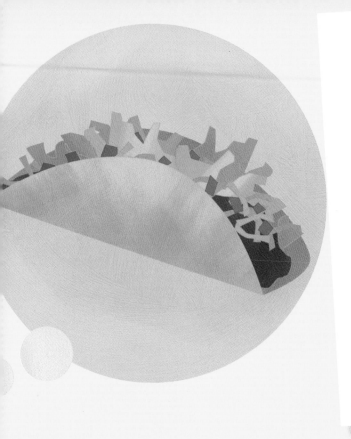

April 3

I wonder what's for lunch today. I smell tacos but I thought tacos were on the menu for tomorrow. Yum yum yum yum I'm so hungry I could eat a horse. What a weird saying I mean who could eat a horse? Who would want to? Oh look DeVon's chewing on his pencil. I suppose I won't be able to chew on my pencil when I get my braces. Getting braces is going to be weird I wish I didn't have to get them.

A journal can help with **DECISION MAKING.** You can brainstorm for ideas, then list the pros and cons of the choices you have. When you see your ideas written down, it might be easier to make up your mind. Here Riley has made a list of four gift ideas. After looking at the pros and cons, the choice seems clear.

April 5

There's a big party at Aunt Jessie's house next week.
Grandma Dee is turning 70. I need to get her a present!

IDEA	PRO	CON
school picture of me	easy to wrap	already has one
chocolate-covered cherries	her favorite treat	gave them last year
perfume	she likes it	already has a bunch
gift certificate for an afternoon of board games	we can do together	???

Gift certificate it is! Maybe include her favorite tea?
Cookies, too. The ones with the butterscotch chips.
I'll ask Mom to help.

April 9

When I grow up, I think I'd
like to live in the mountains.
I still remember our trip to
Colorado. I was 5. Driving
up Pikes Peak was so
awesome. I remember seeing shadows
from the clouds. The air was cold and
felt kind of sharp when I breathed it in.
If I lived in Colorado, maybe I could drive
one of those giant snowplows in the winter.
That would be great!

~ Tool 6 ~

A journal is a private place to write about your **HOPES AND DREAMS.** You might not be comfortable sharing these kinds of thoughts with your friends and family. But in your journal, your dreams are safe.

17

~ Tool 7 ~

In a journal, you can write whatever way you'd like. Maybe **POETRY** would express your thoughts best. Poetry comes in many forms. Try a few, and see what works best for you.

18

April 14

Asked Mom for a sleepover with Sam again. She told me she was tired of my begging and I had to come up with a more creative way to ask. We've been learning about acrostics in school. Maybe a poem will work with Mom. I'll try.

Sam's my best friend

Let him sleep over

Eating chips until the bag is

Empty

Please, please, please

Orange pop

Very late

Eggs and pancakes for breakfast

Repeat next weekend at Sam's house!!

April 16

Xavier taught me this drawing trick today. Pretty cool.

1. Start with a box

2. Add 4 lines

3. Add 4 more lines

4. Add 4 arcs

5. Now add 4 big arcs and connect everything together.

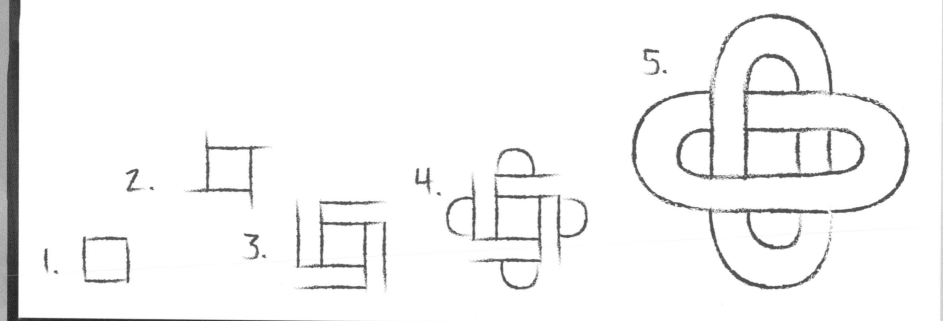

Journals don't have to be just about writing. You can include **DRAWINGS**, too. They can be quick doodles, sketches, maps, or diagrams.

21

April 19

This is from my sleepover with Sam. I think he's still got pieces of chips in his hair.

My spelling bee trophy! I keep it in my bookcase. I won by spelling "Massachusetts."

~ Tool 9 ~

Your journal can include **KEEPSAKES** from the events you're writing about. Ticket stubs, programs, cards, photos— go ahead and tape these items into your journal. Someday you'll be glad you did.

~ Tool 10 ~

Some people like to keep journals with different **THEMES.** These journals are about the same subject. For example, you might keep a separate journal for the trips you take. You could keep one for holidays, or to record ideas for stories or poems. In addition to his everyday journal, Riley keeps a dream journal. He writes all his dreams in it.

24

April 22

Last night, I dreamt I was in a small room with two camels. They were standing with each leg in a bucket of water! One camel looked at me with big brown eyes. Then it slowly started stepping out of the buckets. When I woke up, I was thirsty. Weird!

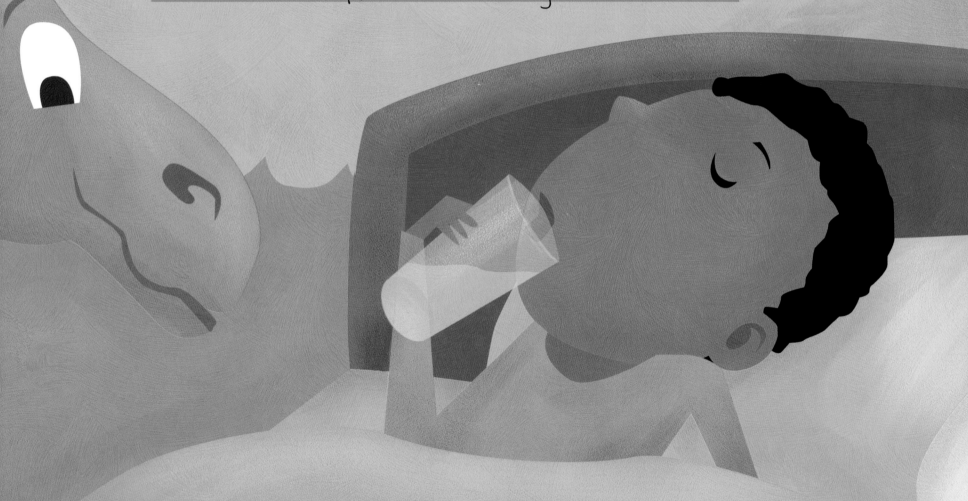

One of the best things about keeping a journal is that you can see how you've changed over time. It reminds you of things you may have forgotten. A journal is a way of writing a letter to your future self.

April 23

I just found my old journal from first grade. I mixed up my d's and b's all the time and I made my q's backward. I said I wanted to walk dogs when I grew up. Maybe I can still do that in the summer. In the winter I'll be out in the snow with my snowplow, clearing the roads in Colorado!

My trip to Colorado Springs

1st Place

my blue ribbon from the science fair

my project was about how rainbows are made

27

Let's Review!

These are the **10 TOOLS** you need to write a great journal.

A journal is the perfect place to record your **OBSERVATIONS (1)**. Writing down your **EMOTIONS (2)** can be like talking to a good friend.

If you get stuck and can't think of anything to write in your journal, try using **WRITING PROMPTS (3)** or **FREE WRITING (4)**.

A journal can help you with **DECISION MAKING (5)**. First brainstorm for ideas and then list their pros and cons. Seeing these lists on the pages of your journal can make the decision clear. A journal is also a safe place to record your **HOPES AND DREAMS (6)**.

Sometimes writing **POETRY (7)** might be the best way to express your thoughts. But journals don't have to be just about writing. They can include **DRAWINGS (8)** and **KEEPSAKES (9)**, too.

Some journals are about one subject or **THEME (10)**. Dreams, holidays, travel, or after-school activities could all be the subject of a theme journal.

Getting Started Exercises

- Can't think of anything to write? Try answering some of these questions: Who is your hero, and why? What famous person would you most like to meet? How would your life be different if you could fly? If you had three wishes, what would they be?

- Carry around a small notebook. When something happens that you want to write about, jot down a few reminder words. Then use those notes when you sit down to write in your journal.

- Sometimes it's easier to write if you feel like you're writing *to* someone—even if that person will never see your journal. You can write to a friend, a parent or grandparent, a teacher, or anyone else. Pretend you're talking to that person, and get writing.

- Write at the same time every day or week. That way, writing will become a good habit.

Writing Tips

 If you are writing on a computer, be sure to save your work. Back up your files often. (Ask your parents or teacher if you don't know how.) That way, if you have computer problems, you won't lose your entire journal. It's also a good idea to print it out regularly. Put the pages in a folder, or a sturdy binder.

 When you look over your journal, you might not like everything you've written. You might want to tear out some pages—but don't! Accept your journal the way it is. Your journal is a record of who you are at a certain time. Someday those pages might teach you something about yourself.

 Remember, no one is judging your journal on how well you write. Your journal is by you, for you. If you're writing a journal for class, and there's something you don't want your teacher to see, label it. Your teacher should respect your wishes.

Glossary

acrostic—a poem in which the first letters of each line spell a word that is the subject of the poem

brainstorm—to come up with lots of ideas all at once, without stopping to judge them

decision—the result of making up your mind about something

emotions—feelings

express—to say or show

free writing—writing whatever pops into your head, without stopping

journal—a written record of thoughts, feelings, and experiences

keepsake—an object that reminds us of a person or event

observations—things that we notice or study

program—a paper that lists the order of events in a performance, such as a band concert or play

prompt—something that gets you started

pros and cons—reasons for (pros) and against (cons) doing something

theme—the main idea of something

To Learn More

More Books to Read

Jackson, Ellen. *My Tour of Europe: By Teddy Roosevelt, Age 10.* Minneapolis: Millbrook Press, 2003.

King, Penny. *Start Writing About Things I Do.* Mankato, Minn.: Chrysalis Education, 2001.

Park, Barbara. *Top-Secret, Personal Beeswax: A Journal by Junie B. (And Me!).* New York: Random House Books for Young Readers, 2003.

Internet Sites

FactHound offers a safe, fun way to find Internet sites related to this book. All of the sites on FactHound have been researched by our staff.

Here's all you do:
Visit *www.facthound.com*
FactHound will fetch the best sites for you!

www.FACTHOUND.com

Index

Look for all of the books in the Writer's Toolbox series:

It's All About You: Writing Your Own Journal
Just the Facts: Writing Your Own Research Report
Make Me Giggle: Writing Your Own Silly Story
Once Upon a Time: Writing Your Own Fairy Tale

Share a Scare: Writing Your Own Scary Story
Show Me a Story: Writing Your Own Picture Book
Sincerely Yours: Writing Your Own Letter
Words, Wit, and Wonder: Writing Your Own Poem